EVERYDAY
I WILL
REMEMBER

Christopher Kuhl

Everyday I Will Remember
Copyright © 2019 **Christopher Kuhl**

bookgini
1603 Capitol Ave, Suite 310,
Cheyenne, WY 82001
www.bookgini.com
1-888-323-7009

ISBN (Paperback): 978-1-64345-315-6
ISBN (Ebook): 978-1-64345-388-0

Printed in the United States of America

ACKNOWLEDGEMENTS

There are so many people to thank as these stories stretch back decades ago, but I'm only now telling them in poetry. I would especially like to thank my family, all of whom involved are now dead. I wish I could have known them, and all the six million.

And I would like to thank the following for their writing support: Frank Rutledge, Lynne C. Handy, Eric Bodwell, and Jen May of Open Sky Poets; Anne Veague, who got me involved with the monthly Waterline Writers reading performances as a featured writer; Kevin Moriarity, who helped me prepare the manuscript for submission to Stratton Press, the publisher of this book; Writer's Relief and my team there for getting my poems out into the larger world; my team at Stratton Press, who did a beautiful job on my book, *Blood and Bone, River and Stone: Memoirs of Lewis County*. I'd also like to thank all my friends far and wide who are not writers, but were willing to read as regular people, and give me their comments and questions. My feeling is that if I'm incomprehensible to an ordinary person who has no more than a good high school or college education, and likes to read, I've failed somehow in my work. As far as this goes, I especially want to thank Beverly Sperry, reader extraordinaire.

Thanks also to the Limestone Coffee and Tea House, for their support. It's my favorite spot to write, and they keep me well supplied with treats and gallons of coffee. I'd especially like to thank Mo, Dennis, Parker, Leah and Joy who've made it the best coffeehouse in town.

Finally, I'd like to thank my good friend Fr. Mike Rasicci; my friends Monica Sisco and Brian Rooney; and my Uncle Paul (my father's youngest brother), for our times and talk together about everything from *The Simpsons* to family matters and spiritual matters. They are truly holy people, and I have learned a great deal from them about who I am as a human being and in relation to the six million.

Shalom.

In memory of my grandmother, Elfriede,
my mother, Sirje,
and all the rest of my family, who did not survive

CONTENTS

PART 1:
THE
HOLOCAUST

PHOTOGRAPH: BALTIC SEA (BETWEEN THE WARS)

I am looking at a family picture
taken on a beach on the Baltic Sea,
where the family had a dacha. The date

is 1937 or '38, and I only ever knew
two of those pictured: my grandmother,
who died in 1967 when I was eleven,

and my mother, still living. The rest
died in the war and Stalin's purges.

How did this picture survive?

They're looking into the sun:
my uncle Verder's eyes are squinting,
his head slightly turned; my great-grandmother's

are simply shut. The wind is blowing,
whipping up the pale sea behind them,
and the women's, and my mother's bobbed hair

is blowing off to the side. (Perhaps my great-grandmother's eyes
are shut because of the wind, too.)

They're all in swimming togs,

except my great-grandparents:
she is wearing a print dress and sandals,
he is in striped trousers, braces, a long-sleeved white shirt,
and holds a hat. My grandmother,

who must be twenty-four or 'five,
is in high heels even though she's wearing a swim suit,
and she holds a float shaped like a frog:

is that for my mother?

    The more I look at this picture,

the more I see resemblances: great-aunt Leida
looks like her father; my mother now looks like her mother then;
I look like my grandfather, Toivo. And when I look

at the back of the picture, where my mother has written
names and dates, my heart seizes for a moment:
these vibrant people on a summer beach in 1937 or '38,

and the terrible cataclysm of dates:

1886-39 Leida
1915-41 Arvo
1911-42 Pia
1934-43 Merike
1914-45 Toivo

EVERY DAY I WILL REMEMBER

What is the truth?
At the Nuremberg trials
For crimes against humanity,
A Nazi pleads his innocence:

I did no harm: I was just
An accountant behind a desk,
Making sure all prisoners were

Accounted for. Our soldiers
Packed the people in the ovens
Neat and tight as bricks,

Gassed and burned them. The soldiers
Brought me the numbers every day of bodies
Piled at the bottom of the electric

Fence, finding a hopeless freedom
In suicide. I didn't tell them
To do it; I just made

The relevant notes in the ledgers.
What could I do? I was
Just an accountant; it wasn't

As though they were people that
Mattered. And I was so tired.
As the crematoria worked through

The night, the insomniac stars
Were blinded, diminished by fire.
And the prisoners? They

Were reduced to bone fragments
And muddy ash. Other prisoners
Mucked out the crematoria;

I also kept track of their work hours
And deaths on the job. If I didn't do it,
Some other accountant would have.

It wasn't my fault. I was
Just an accountant following orders.
I didn't do anything wrong.
I wasn't responsible.

An Allied Soldier Upon Liberating the Camps

The mud I slosh through
Is all that remains of
Grandparents, fathers, mothers,
Sisters, brothers. I vomit.

When the camps are liberated,
There is no cheering, no shouting
Mazel tov! There is only silence:
The living skeletons do not know

What has happened. But then
One hand rises in a blessing,
And soon a few more, and then

Almost everybody who has
Strength. Once prisoners, now
Refugees, they are given clothes,
Boots, blankets. They are also given

Food and chocolate, but they are
So weak, translucent almost, they can
Take only a little food, a little tea.

Are they happy? Surely they must be.

But they weep. Even the soldiers.
All of them, weeping.
Weeping.

AGON

" . . . where can I escape, flying to the bright air or sea?"
Orestes

this was the long turn the long road
the black road turning into the black wood
the pine wood pokeweed black as the black water
as the black water weeds in the swollen river
the thick serried water—
this was the long turn this was the way it had to begin . . .

this was the long turn falling like the last thought
turning deep into the long night the black cold turning
into itself into its thick black center the lurid air
dank and festering its black smell smeared in the black night
congealed in the black wood clotted like the black water weeds
in the swollen river turning in the bright wounded air

turning the way the earth turned deep in the long night
turning in the black wood silent in the deep night turning
like the festering river turning in its lurid center turning
turning in the torn and swollen air—
the bright bloody air turning to itself weeping like the sea

LOST, 1941

I.

crashing through the woods
dense as an internment camp

screaming

soul reduced to ashes—

brother,

bring me home

II.

the supermoon shines
rising in the eastern sky

smoke, grit:

a train rolls through

III.

a spark of fire quickening
threatening

in the night

in the night:

my heart contracts—

the dark snap of a raven biting through bone—

BRAMBLY QUESTIONS

(inspired by sam sax)

How do you know
you exist? That

you're alive
in a box in a parking

lot? Well, you are
unless someone opens

the box in the blazing
sun: then you're dead.

(what is this place where
sun and earth meet and

live boys are scattered
about in boxes?)

How do you know
you exist and are not

just a pile of bones
in a mass grave? Well,

you do if
someone calls out

and you respond

SOMETHING TO THINK ABOUT

There are things you can
think about,
and things you can't.

There are ordinary
miracles, and
then there are fabulous

miracles. The Resurrection
is a miracle
that cannot be seen

or understood: people rise
from the dead
all the time; everyone

sees them sometime
or other. Moses,
on the other hand, was

an ordinary man,
leader of the Exodus,
inconceivable as the stream

he sent rushing through
the desert by striking a rock.
He was always

bargaining with God
on behalf of the people,
God's recalcitrant people.

Miraculously, he reached
The Promised Land, but could not
go in with his people.

In his old age, homeless, he
died, and was buried in a long-
lost, forgotten grave.

Think about it.

THE END OF THE DAY

You were ten once, twenty,
Even forty, although you couldn't
Believe it then, let alone remember it.

Now pushing seventy, you see
The previously invisible elderly,
Shadows, dust motes, skulls

Visible under the shrunken flesh.

    You can tell

Just by looking
That they're a little tired,
Maybe even in these last fragile years

Exhausted. Now reality hits:
Although you've never been much

For prayers, you now say them
Daily, nightly, because the next breath
Might be your last,

Or you really might not wake to the new day's sky.

OUR IRON HOUSES

We cast shadows; therefore we are.

We live in iron houses;
We die in iron ovens, sweating
In our insignificance on
A dying planet. The absence

Of the sun is also the absence
Of shadow is the absence
Of trees, rivers, is the absence
Of ourselves, trapped

In one another's otherness,
Accommodated by bone,
Shadows burned in stone.

Yet still the moon
Loves us, going around
And around coolly, without
Searing us like the sun's
Unbearable heat:

Who can say at what precise point
Dying begins? Or death ends?

A man remembers a bulldozer
On the edge of a mass grave.
A woman remembers the newly
Blessed leaven. Even children
Remember Chanukah's dreidel,
Noisemakers at Purim, and weep.

Miles apart, fire and water,
No bread, no meat. Here
Is everywhere. Jewish souls
Are saints martyred. We live
And die in iron houses.

TIME'S MOAT

Rain threading through trees,
bending tangled plants,
prying the slabs of diminishing
daylight apart. The rain

makes a moat to keep out, protect
against foreigners,
thieves,

but I find only my
self reflected in the water:
am I the outsider trying
to get in? Was I left?

Or did I choose to leave? Nothing
is as far as here: the past
has, depending on what you

believe, a knowable unknowable
beginning. The now is eternal.
And the future doesn't exist at all.

A BLESSING

In ancient times,
Infants ate butter and honey
Until they were of an age

To eat bread. This was the way
Of things. Now

The infants have grown, and
There is no butter, no honey.
Instead, they have seen blood

Where there should be no blood,
Bones scattered where once
There was life. And so it goes.

O, threshed and winnowed ones,
Rise up from the earth and know
That you are worth more to Me

Than a thousand sparrows.

Rise up in this stained December
Twilight, and know that you
Are loved, blessed beyond measure.

Rise up! Rise up!

BLOOD

Some people have a taste

For blood.

If I could, I would eat
The whole world, quaff
The seasoned universe.

And it wouldn't matter:
I would be nothing more
Than dust in the wind's fingers,

Splinters of rock on the edge
Of a twisted mountain road.

SHADOWS

In the straining dark of
night, the sky cluttered
with stars, shadows

wander the house, touching
things, their shadowy boneless fingers
unable to grab, pick up, and put

objects down again,

so nothing is disturbed: a wrist watch,
an empty tea cup, a dusty pair of
wingtips

beside the bed where the couple
sleeps inside each other's warm,
moist

but ever-barren breath.
There is no future here to carry on;
and those of us watching

laugh until we weep.

DESECRATION

God made humankind
From dust,
In His own image.

    Millennia later,

Humans put into place
The Final Solution,
Reducing God's created images

Into dust and ash.

    I ask the sky,

What is humankind?
Does God dwell in us,
Or we in Him? Did the snake

Bite the Nazis' heels?

CONFLAGRATION

Unseeing eyes see extinct stars.

The first faces of hell. Death.

No shadow = no strength to live.

The officers in their stone coats watch.

We *are* shadows. Do we live?

The knife-blue twilight.

The sky hovering over a pit of tangled bones.

What is it to die at the hands of men? Some men know, but those of us still living are woefully innocent, naïve, and there's no one left to ask. I weep: I so want to know, but the dead, hearts rotted away long ago, hoard their secrets and refuse to the depths of their bones, the depths of the earth, to share. Or do they not know, too? Is it just an inexplicable part of being, non-being?

A blinding shaft of light burns on the mad dance of the Jews.

NIGHT LIFE

I am not myself.
Nobody is. We are refugees,
living

in a black forest,
alone, yet together—
still lonely, even so.
When a dog howls,

join in: the arms
of the wind will embrace
you.

NOTHING AT ALL

What is it like
to be dead? Is it
dramatic, the swirling
colors

of sunsets and oceans?
Is it dull, the ground-
covering leaves once
vibrant,

but now so wet and black
so heavy even the wind
can't move them?

I don't know. Maybe
death is all these things
or maybe it's nothing at all.

So I'll settle for a life and
death as simple and pale
as a beginning, middle
and end

but that end not so simple
as we pray for. Fire
and ash. Fire

and ash.

An Old Man Remembers the Child

To reverse history's flow,
I drink from sour ponds.
I do not know where my family is,

Or even if I had one.
Now, I resist signs of affection
Because I will surely die,
My long soul laments.

My thigh bones snap;
Eventually my brain will slide
From my skull

(Because I will die).

Bar mitzvah boy, I join
The day that will never
Return. We hide in the darkest
Hours, with no light,

No food. We eat leaves,
Grass; we eat the acorns
Left by the pigs:

I crack a tooth, but tell
No one: the Sons of Mengele
Will search me out, conduct
Tests, experiments,

And then I am thrown half-
Aware of where I am:
The burn pile. From

Morning's first breath
To last, is one forever day.

*

The crematoria chimneys blow
Grey smoke, the announcement
Of sheer evil,

Unlike the Vatican's white smoke
Announcing a new Pope,
A good man, a kind man, praying
For us all, even Jews, even though
There's no way to be sure
In this soul-stricken place.

*

It is always this time;
The time that we live by
In this time. From eighteen
Months to ninety-four years,
We walk every day; it

Averages out to 34,675 days,
All, for all practical purposes,

The same: at ninety-four
What else is there to change?
In my old brain, small faces
Line abandoned streets.

I lived here once, maybe
Never, forever,
Never. Always I echo the howl

Of loss, and stare blindly
At the broad moon on water.

GOD SPEAKS

I write of end things:
the terrifying hunger,
the thin bones. The last time:

street kids standing
on the bones and stones
of their ancestors, history

merely a cemetery that
has to be approved (no flippant headstones),
every turn in the path

a memory, the day's measure
of the past, sorrow
in the wind. The whitewashed tombs

are beautiful on the outside
but inside, full of corruption
and dead men's bones.

Life proceeds, enrages;
God, speak for the silenced man

THE PEOPLE

The hobbled, beaten, worn out
To the edge of death,
Haggard from standing
For hours barely clothed
In tatters of the dead's
Remaining bits and pieces,
No coats, shoes, hollow-eyed,
Have one reaction when the
Camps are liberated:

They collapse in the
In the ashy snow.

Then a single voice
Whispers:

Earth, have mercy;
Do not abandon me . . .

SEQUENCE

1
I wake in the night
to the smell of baking bread;
warmed, I drift back to sleep

2
a path
I don't know where it goes,
but I walk to find out

3
zero visibility
ashes so thick we meet
ourselves and do not know

4
I spend days recuperating
from myself, looking forward
to night, a single candle and a dream

5
stone soup: a pebble,
bones, roots, leaves:
a winter night's supper

6
what do we remember? the ovens
and the souls freed up in smoke,
ashes as light as a single rose petal

7
all grief is ageless; breathe,
breathe while you still can

OFFERING

Beings of clay,
we are born into this
life and we die from

this life. Christ's blood
in its violence splattered
his mother's robe as she mourned

beneath him. We are,
all of us, splattered
with blood whether

Jew or Christian:
this is the holocaust:
we are the burnt offerings

to the Fascist gods...

Monochrome

gray. mud.
gray mud. ash.
ashes floating
in a thick gray
slurry of river.
gray. gray stones.
jaw bones. gray.
hiding in the woods
the gray woods, eating
dead gray animals,
gray trees
damp leaves gray
with mold. in the camp,
gray soup. a pebble, one
bit of gray potato, in a
tin cup, cold, gray.
shaved gray heads, lice,
gray skin, death gray
from typhus. women
in gray dresses, gray
men in gray striped
tattered pajamas. all
the gray effects
of the jews in gray
boxes. a gray,
minor shadowed
infraction

and the silver flash
of a bayonet gray
between ribs visible
in gray, broken, broken
gray dead bodies

MADNESS ROAMING

I feel the heaviness of rain
On the leaves, wedges

Of damp moonlight, waves
Crashing on the north sea's edge.

A hurricane gathers itself up,
Its eye blind as the Cyclops,

Blind, ferocious:
We know the thunder, the hail,

Even the tornadoes may herald
Its coming. We dream, in

And out of our bodies; time
Moves back and forth in

The dark air. What will we save?
What will we leave behind?

Nothing, everything:

    Nothing

But neighborhoods of ghosts,
The newly dead roaming.

BEFORE I WAS BORN
(BUT CANNOT FORGET)

Mass graves in the forest. Those
Who can still stand wield a shovel,
Pushing the bodies into bloody,
Muddy, suppurating, helter-skelter
Piles. The dead, their souls

Torn from their bodies, never to return,
Live in the shadows of another world,
A black hole, starving for the light.

All the world is at war,
Yet not everybody realizes the
Atrocities going on from Germany to Poland,
China to Russia, to the Ukraine and Japan.
Not just Jews and troops and POWs,
But others, their plain lives snatched
Away, sixty to eighty million
Dead.

Dead. Still, when I visit Yad Vashem
And see the thousands of artifacts,
And the dome covered with pictures
Of the murdered Jews, something inside me
Breaks: How can I say these words?

Glorified and sanctified be God's great name
Throughout the world which He has created
*According to His will...*ya-da ya-da ya-da...
How can I believe?

I stand in the center and scream,
And hear the cattle cars creaking again,
Laden with those already lost, too numb
To cry, to pray.

INSANITY

A Nazi officer's testimony
At the Nuremberg trials.

"It wasn't us. It was
The Jews, six million of them
Bonding

Together into one massive
Dragon, breathing long trails
Of smoke

Pounding across the land,
Devoted not to their God

But dedicated to suffocating,
Burning the master race."

A SURVIVOR SPEAKS

I am a Jew.
I was a Jew. Now
I am a number, recycled.
I have forgotten the name
My parents gave me. I do not
Remember my Hebrew name:
God has forgotten us;
I have forgotten God.

Things are no better
When the Allies break
The camps. We continue
To be inmates in another,
Refugee camp. Yet
They also know us only as
Numbers. We are blind:
We have seen too much:

Worked, overworked,
A cup of gray soup
Once a day: "worked
To extermination."
Abused in ways inconceivable.
Once, a woman maybe six months
Along, came in on
A transport: as they

Were sorted out—death, hard labor—
A soldier screamed at her
And with his rifle, slammed
The back of her knees,

And she fell, confused,
Terrified. The soldier
Screamed again: get up!
Slowly, she got to her feet,

Holding her belly. The soldier
Grabbed a butcher's knife,
Ripped her open, and speared
The fetus up for everyone
To see: "Gut, ja?" The troops
Laughed, but the Jews
Were silent. Genocide
Was familiar in Jewish history,

But that was then, and this
Was now. The woman was
Dragged to the death line,
The soldier threw the baby
On a pile of rocks, which
Those chosen for hard labor
Were ordered to smash. Moses
Struck a rock, and water

Gushed forth. Here, men
In striped clothes struck
The rocks and they brought
Forth blood. And then
The woman was screaming.
Another soldier struck her belly
Again, and then shot her.
She didn't live long enough

To forget her name, and
Because she was destined
For the gas chambers,
She was not tattooed.

Small blessings.

But why did I survive?

I was strong, silent, obedient.
I did what I was told to do,
Without complaint. Digging
Mass graves for the gassed bodies
And pushing them in, I did not
Even say Kaddish. Why
Did I survive? Because
Of dumb luck. God

Had nothing to do with it,
No more than a golden calf,
Baal. Maybe someday,
I will be able to say again,

I am a Jew.

FROM COSMOS TO CHAOS

Spirea bushes grapple
with the house, milking it until

it has no color, the foundation
crumbling until the bushes

flower all the colors of white.
A dog barks and the first star

flares up. I do not know
my plants; my mother tells me.

I do not know my stars;
my mother tells me. And then

she flogs me, gleefully angry,
flogs me as the soldiers did her

for the universal chaos
such ignorance creates. God

created order, perfect, to be
worshipped,

      and you call yourself a Jew,

a human being?

Look where you are, extermination
looming, a present without beginning—or

            end—

THE MUD AND BONE GARDEN

He was to die somewhere
Near a Polish camp. From
Whose bullet? And for whose
Reward? An inmate's?
A pretty young girl, Katrina's? A young
Soldier with dogs? About them
He knew nothing.

History lasted
In that moment when he was
Breaking bread and drinking wine:

Theirs are wastelands
And rusty tracks through the woods.
Rail switches frozen stiff as stone
Seventy years ago, when all the men,
Women, children were reduced
To transparency and dense
Ash ground to a muddy slurry:

The purple-black garden
Of human bones.

BUTCHER

The houses, in little
clutches, have their windows
darkened. Nobody

ventures forth, where
once they were good neighbors.
Something is happening:

a single person,
a whole family, disappears
with no one left

to tend the garden,
collect the chickens' eggs.
As the days go on,

the streets are empty:
the baker bakes for nobody;
the butcher, cutting

chops, roasts, steaks,
is uneasy: he hears whispers
that the Germans

are doing their own
butchering; he doesn't know
whether it's true or

what it could possibly
mean: the villages are gone,
the streets running

with blood, a shattering
in the air, a long, hard
winter expected.

IN THE BLEAK MIDWINTER

These are the darkest days.
Hazy sun, night skies dominating
The hours of these holy days,
The earth turning down
And into itself. My body

Is a hollow core,
Implacably cold. The fire
Cracks, losing its luster,
Nothing more than brittle air.

Breathe, breathe:

We have grown too old
For whispering, but too old also
For crying out. The mother
Gives birth to nothing but

Wind. In these last

Few moments before death,
We do not know how or if
To say goodbye. All the universe
Pulses as do we: let us
Close our eyes, take one more

Breath, and dying, awake
In the land of the cold east wind.

EARTH, MOON, FIRE

The earth has an old man's
Smell,
The moon an old woman's.

Every now
And then I have a soul,
Especially

During the day, when I
Pray upon waking,
Thanking God for returning

My soul to me
Another day. Every day
The earth

And sun swing around
Each other,
Running all of us through

The galaxy
And its whipping tail. March on,
Old man,

Old woman: the world has got
To end sometime,
Somewhere. In the end

The blood sun
Will burn in the west, and in
The morning

The truth will be we old men,
Old women,
With our musty smell will not

Have our souls
Returned to us; there will be

No prayers left;

Nowhere left to set our feet
Except in fields
Of the Devil's liquid fire.

EVOLUTION

An inch of wheat field
Tousled by the wind;

A weed clinging tenuously
To a pile of stones,

Then torn off in the storm.

    We are born

To arrive
As we are born to leave:

Naked arriving,
Naked leaving.

Our skin has no pockets:
We won't need house keys

Where we're going.

UNSEEN

Is God already here?
Transparent, but not invisible?
We only

Can see what is solid.
For instance,

We cannot see the sky,
Only sun, moon, stars, clouds,
When actually

The sky meets, surrounds
Our feet; invisible,

We can only see our feet,
Dust covered, standing
Still.

INVENTORY

Neatly separated and piled
Shirts, pants, blouses, skirts,
And dresses, old hats, gloves, once

Glamorous coats and suits,
And eighty-nine pairs of shoes:
Muddied, torn soles flapping

And the feet that once fit
These precisely lined-up shoes
Also gone—

The footbone connected to
The ankle bone, the ankle bone
Connected to the leg bone, to

The knee bone, hip bone, etc.—
Some hidden, wrapped
In leaves, bark, tied with vines,

Or gone entirely, lost along with
The bodies they once grounded,
Grounded in the thick black ash

Of midnight, blinded by the
Ever-blazing camp lights,
With nowhere to hide,

And only one place to go—

ORIGINS

Wandering loosely through
my dreams,
the dead lie oblivious

in the old, still yard
on the hill,
whispering to the living

who walk beneath
the blood-red moon, saying,
Tell me,

Where am I from?
What tribe lays claim
To my face?

Do tribes share
bones—femur, tibia, fibula,
vertebrae—

do they share,
or eat one another, rich
stew with spicy blood gravy?

Tell me: where am I from?
A bone is a key
to my motherland, my people,

a key from a rib scraped clean
from its cage protecting the red,
pounding fist

deep in my people's chests,
too frail to turn a lock against
the winds that wail

from far-off worlds,
my shadow rustling in alien
lands. Tell me again,

where am I from,
among the living and the dead?

POSTCARD: WHERE WE LIVE

We live in the darkening
world of the air;
the bruised moon shivering
naked, a terrible wonder:

where is a safe place
to hide in this smoky
November nightfall?

At the edge of the west,
we linger almost east
among the mountains,
and wonder what it would
be like to live somewhere beyond,

    floating in the flaring

west winter winds . . .

The Bottom of Midnight

We live at the bottom
of midnight, trying
to breathe as the guards
beat us with fiery rods,
heads, shoulders, backs;
we try not to scream
as the rods are heated
over and over to sticks
of fire, branding us, burning
us, flaying us, until our skin
is no more than battered
parchment, peeling
burnt, broken flesh off
in ragged sheets through the long
hours of death in the cold,
blind dawn.

IDENTITY

My real name is Abraham.
Yesterday my name was Jew.
Today my name is A-1778.
Tomorrow my name will be grave-digger.
My name once was human.
Secretly, I know my name is Child of God.

EPITAPH

dead
i become only
the space
i've left behind

a door ajar
as night crawls
creeps

in

PART 2: AFTER THE WAR

GATHERING STORMS

Twilight. We drive home,
The clouds gathering, heat
Lightning in the distance.
We listen to the radio's static:
Nobody speaks.

AFTER THE WAR

Back in the old country
zaydehs and bubbes
plant root vegetables

and lay their dead
sons on top for plant
food and then

cover all with wet
earth. Someday,
we all must eat.

Toivo's Ring

I notice wedding bands,
The bonding of a handsome
Young couple in love. And then,

One night at dinner
Axes split the front door
And heavily armed Bolsheviks
Burst in, howling, screaming

Even as the child screams.

Toivo calmly passes his ring
To his wife before he is kicked,
Shoved at gun point,
Beaten and stabbed, stumbling
Into the dark, gone forever—

Remember me, remember me,
My love, but oh, forget my fate—

And so my mother
Passed the ring on to me:
A single son, I wear it
As if I were married.

It's all I have:
Siilaberg, Siilametz, Myim:
A whole tribe wiped out
Except for Elfriede and Sirje,
Lost in America, and soon
Dead.

Tribeless, then, who am I?
Except for the ring, with *Fritzi*
And the wedding date inscribed,
I am the last of the line,

An echo of what was once love,
Now overcome forever
By rifles, starvation and Zyklon B.

Vow

I brought my son, Levi,
Twelve years old,
Into the camps. We were both

Assigned to labor, but in
Separate areas. I saw him
Only occasionally, but I

Could see he was surviving:
Starving, but still alive
In his tattered striped pajamas.

When we were freed and
Reunited, he was stiff, silent:
No hugging, no yelling, no tears.

    And I vowed

In that moment, I would never
Bring another child into this world.
I have kept my vow:

My son died shortly after
The war: his skeleton collapsed
From starvation. I was stricken,

But did not cry. Instead,
I continue to live his stiffness,
His silence, and live on scraps

I find on the streets. This
Is war's eternal legacy.

IMMIGRANTS

We have met the enemy and he is us.
Walt Kelly, POGO

The country we live in
Is not the country
We would choose to live in.

We want to live
In a land of husky,
Broad-leaved trees;
On mountains as distant
As the curving of the Earth.

We do not want to live
Among the wicked
Who are like the tossing sea
That cannot keep still.

We are still alone
Who love the dead beneath
The rind of the moon, leaves
Falling as the autumnal equinox
Approaches. The abject poverty

Of dirt surrounds us
Here in this unwanted country:
Our humanness betrays us
Like a cage; we eat

The worms beneath the earth,
Crunch the crickets and praying mantis,
Hiding ourselves beneath a makeshift altar.

ONCE A CHILD

Sixty years old
And I want to talk
To my mother. She

Would be eighty now,
But she's been long dead:
If she could, would she

Want to talk to me?
If she could,
Would I be able to

Hear her? Maybe not.
Maybe it's failing hearing.
Or maybe her jaws

Have dropped, her tongue
Disintegrated, unable
To speak. I

Don't know: I
Stand above her on the turf,
Ashamed,

Ashamed because I've
Disappointed her, fallen
Short. One

Of us is mortal,
The other not.

SUICIDE: THE WIND

The wind whispers
its few small truths
to the earth: dreamers,

how much truth can any
of us
tolerate? I jumped

off a bridge once,
and was reborn, wise
as a body's worth of ashes:

it seemed the only option
after surviving the War
alone. Now

I am like everyone I knew:
stateless, nameless, keenly
aware that everywhere

I have been, or am, or even
will be,
God is absent, asleep somewhere,

and I have always been dead,
or like the wind, never born.

YAD VASHEM

During days of remembrance
we gather at Yad Vashem,

and see colors spinning in the
dark light, but not really:

we've just been taught what
the colors are; what we really see

are black and white photos
meant to suggest an airless antiquity,

as though the events occurred thousands
of years earlier, but really happened

only two generations ago,
and in which we all—the dead,

the survivors, their descendants,
are, with the rest of the world, complicit.

got mukhl mir ikh hobn gazindikt. *

*God forgive me for I have sinned. (Yiddish)

WIND, ASHES

No matter our age, our lives are
indigenous to the ashes of memory,
our parents and grandparents,
aunts, uncles, cousins—

their ashes too;

until all of us, those in the war
and their children
born in the new country, where
they are citizens by virtue of birth,

but their forebears are not;
their ashes, their memories mixed
with a bit of Jerusalem dirt
are scattered into the west wind,

originating from the distant, unknown
territories and running
east across the Atlantic, back
to the motherland.

KADDISH

There's a spirit in a room,
In my solitary mind.

Yesterday it rained all day;
Today everything is steamy,

The eucalyptus, black, breathes
Its life force into the greenery,

And I feel my spirit rising
Within the one day allotted for burial.

The coyote comes sniffing around,
Sees the moon, the mourners, and howls

At the twenty-fourth hour.

Original Sin

Death begins and never ends:
the earth continues to spin and by
the end, there may still be some grass
to be on the right side of, as
my uncle always says. That, and
if asked how he's doing, says,
"Living the dream, son, living
the dream." And yet, at eighty-seven,
he loses his cane and balance
and falls into bushes, flower gardens,
vegetable patches, a rabbit's nest.

What I really want to say is that
as the world continues to turn and
its living population diminishes,
the world will be full of graves. Everyone
will be dead except for the two gravediggers
and a mourner dressed in black, davening.
Soon there will be no grass, and God
will weep for his people, his whole
creation. There is nothing but death,
piled in pits, the landscaping
a joke: there never was a Garden of Eden,
a tree of life, no Adam, no Eve, no serpent:
it was all a hoax, just like God, a being
without being.

SUICIDAL THOUGHTS AND ACTIONS

The lights of heaven
press on my head
and what once was darkness
now fires forth as jeweled
as the crown I got on my tooth
yesterday. Will I leave
a legacy when I die
by a speeding hit and run
at the age of fifty-four? Or
fed snail poison by my girl-
friend, turning my insides to ash?
Or stabbed while walking
down the street humming on
cocaine? Or smothered by my
wife for my snoring, depriving
her of deep sleep and dreams?

*

Or will I be a suicide,
jumping from the bridge into
deceptively welcoming water,
but in reality water as smooth
and hard as concrete? Shattered
there, I will leave nothing of value
behind, nothing I value, except
my left-handed fielder's glove:
what will happen to it? My young
nephew will want it "just because"—
no more than that. As I fly
for eight seconds without wings,
I feel my mother's blood

run through my veins.
And then I cry one or two
seconds, gathering speed,
and splatter, splinter,
and then am silent, dead.

THE COMING

So many graves so silent:

A small fenced space of
Certainty. That's all. That's
Enough. It's almost dark,
The moon a slender bit
Of rind. The dead

Are buried heads to the
West in preparation for
Jesus's coming from the
East. The dead rise in
Tight formation, saluting

The face of God. They are
Renewed, redeemed with
Their God-given names.

Be still. Listen. Be watchful.
You are the result of the love
Of thousands, listening
To what speaks in the blood:
You are welcome, free

Of the fog that separates, loses
Contact between earth and the heavens;
God present in the soft nothingness
Of air,

The weighty weightlessness
Of eternity.

MY FATHER THE SINGER

My father is an old man,
old enough to remember
the Holocaust, even though

he was on the other side
of the ocean. He sings

a virile song, widening
for a love he held, a
survivor of the camps,

who spoke no English;
he sings for all that live,

and all that died. When
she died, he sang the song
again, this time almost

brutally: how could God
take her from his arms?

Maybe it would have been
better if she had never joined
with him,

or even survived the war
that tainted them. He wishes

he were a child once again, silent,
selfish, oblivious to the world—

and her.

Sirje Sets the Town on Fire

she didn't

speak English

but she knew the language
that mattered

she was a foreign knock-out

and while the boys
were ogling her

sunning on the rocks

she was saying

in a wordless language
come here boys—arching
her back—

you boys in white t-shirts

and tight Levi's

come

and I teach you

the syntax of sex

FALLING INTO WINTER

The young boy holds
a hand-warmed nickel,
head leaning

into his mother's hip,
clenching his teeth,
torn between desire

and need. They have been
up and in the streets,
effervescent with the remains

of last night's rain, up
for the renaissance of daylight,
hoping to find food, a warm

place, comfort in each other,
someone to teach the boy
the ways of the world—

  although maybe he already knows—

but alone is really just
alone again, and the day has
passed unsuccessfully:

belated as a bruise,
the dark presses in, and
mother and son sigh,

falling into winter.

SOMEWHERE BY THE SEA

I am not a gardener.
I lie on a bed
Of dark sea grass, the wind

Sifting across my body,
Lingering over my legs, ribs,
My hollowed chest, through

My wind-tossed hair. At night,
The sea is cool, placid:
The wind has stopped. Yet still

I lie on the dark sea grass,
In the moonless midnight's
Silence. Slowly,

The earth and I sink together;
We remember floating bright
In the dark waters of the womb.

    Somewhere

In the distance, a candle
Smolders like the scent of grief.

A Mother's Prayer to Her Son: Remember Me

I gather the wind
in the palm

of my hand:

son of my womb,
son of my vows,

you have stirred my
shadow to life:

I am the vine without
a name, wrapped

around a green, green briar

as in old, almost forgotten
ballads and tales –

CARRION

Death invades the bones
Like a hawk's scream. The dead

Are forgetful; living,
They were heartless, poisoned.

Now memory is endless,
Vita brevis. The dust

Flies up, plain and sad
As a small town graveyard.

My blood is unfaithful,
My faith bloodless. A crow

Welcomes me home. No,

No, no! The dead are all a delusion:
Their works are nothing;
Their images are empty wind.

WHAT MATTERS

My mother is dead these fifteen years.
My sister is dead these eight years.

My brother is very much alive,
    Sparks shooting everywhere.

My father is eighty-two, alive
    But frail. He has purple
    Parchment skin.

He has a power wheelchair so he can
    Go out and feel the Carolina sun
    On his shoulders. He lives

Among hard, sharp-edged people,
    Bitter about who said what to whom;
    Who's cheating; whose wife
    Is a bitch. They live

In a small, dilapidated town
    Buildings rotting, peeling skin,
    Looking over the earth's charred edge.

Life goes on, but for how much longer?
    I await the phone call
    That will make me an orphan.

And when it does, I will say,
    alav ha-sholom. *

And friends will say to my brother,
    To me, our tiny family,

Hamakhim yenacham etkhan betokh
        she'ar avalai Tzyonvi ʿYerushalayim.**
The stones will tremble with grief,
        As they have for all time,

And I will take leave of the sun
        And fields, retreating
        To the dark house.

All truth that matters lies in the grave.

*Rest in peace.

**May God console you among the other mourners
of Zion and Jerusalem.

APOLOGY

The light is swallowed
by the barren dark,

God's stars fall
into the last, now dry,
ocean, the trees no longer

dance in the wind—God,
despairing, has ceased
to breathe—

and I am left with
an unheard, meaningless prayer—
"forgive me"—

and ashes on my tongue

STATEMENT

I am

Not guilty.

But one of seven
billion exhausting
the planet, itself

one of billions
in the universe,
some touched by light

from an edge
fourteen billion light-
years away,

I know

I am responsible. So
for the world, past and
present, I will struggle
to swallow—

as must we all—

the terrible beauty of the
dark light of joy and pain.

REFLECTION ON PROVERBS

Perverse: this is not
God's holy fool,
who is pure of heart.

No, this is the fool
who is rebuked, perverse
in the instructions he is

given, but refuses to learn:
he will rest in the assembly
of the dead. His lamp will

go out in the utter darkness.
The stories will come spilling
like bones. Sometimes

all we have of a tale
is its ending, the pages
mostly burned. My body

hums: I see dead boys
marching, dead girls singing:
all we have left

is a field of orphans.

SILENCE, DARK

black hooves owl bones
white pine oak sugar maple
a deer dead by the side of
a silent road

feathers stone frosted ferns
on the windows lit by bright
sheets of moonlight

it is in memory that we
define ourselves the old
stories on the other side
of knowledge bright clots

of blood waves of time
shaping rocks hills valleys
boundaries of distant lakes

gravel roads in an old
gray town and one paved
street with old gray stores
surrounded by dairy farms

corn bean wheat fields
truck gardens shadows lengthened
by the dying light tell me

what color is my fear of the dark

THE EDGE

All Jews know death,
the scent of lost bodies,

fresh graves, the world-wide
diaspora, pushing closer and

closer to the edge, an apparently
capricious God or none,

and the Nazis' Final Solution:
the dark, roaring anvil of death.

We said it could not,

must not, would not—we would never
let it—happen again. But it can,

and with prevalent, centuries
old, unfathomable hatred of Jews

rolling in and over in blood-borne
waves, it begins again

and again across this side of
the waters, the sky falling,

the earth shattering, the children of God
bloody, burnt, crushed,

a swastika on a temple door
in what was supposed to be a new life . . .

MY DOG DEATH

My dog is Death. We take walks
in the long fields of shadows

between the deep land
and the sea, once deep,

but now dry, where only
salt and the copper taste

of blood remain, and in my mind
a tangled heap of bones.

But in this new country,
as Death leads me,

I remember Scripture and feel
his warm, soft coat:

a soft tongue can break bones.*
I will live after all. Omaine.

*Proverbs 25:15

MY CHILDREN

I have crossed the sea
from eastern Europe:
free now, but still a prisoner

in my mind. Here,
hesitant, I have had
a child, two:

the first generation
after the Holocaust.
But it is too much, and

I do not live to hold
my second child. I
have no family, so my children

will disappear, into the
system, their own kind of camp,
never knowing who and what

their mother was.

Now, the rabbi presides
over my burial;
after the last shovelful

of dirt is tossed on
the grave—this final house—
all that is left

is an immense dark space
of noise, tearless weeping.
Who will recognize and free my children?

FRACTURES

The world is fractured. History is fractured. The ecosystem is fractured. Is the universe as we know it fractured? Is there a broken space beyond which there is another universe? Or is it a joke, like the "Fractured Fairytales"? Fractures shape each of us, giving us to do whatever we were meant, and have the desire to do. Yet it is not always what we want or expect.

I criticize the dark, the light; the night, the day; the sun, the moon and the stars. Night seems a betrayal for diurnal people, yet there are people who are nocturnal, by choice of work, or temperament, or a combination: do they take a job because it is a night job, or does the job transform them into a creature of the night?

I am fractured: a Jew, a Christian; introverted, extroverted; an Estonian, an Italian, with a piece missing that would help to heal one of my fractures: conflicted as a Jew by my German blood. I am an ethnic orphan, but embraced by parents who fight and beat each other, and then caress one another with long, broad strokes, and disappear into their room. As a child, I wasn't sure what went on in there, but if it was the master bedroom, who was the master guiding the marital ship?

I am a glutton; I am a skeleton; I scream and I am silent. I am the first generation in this country, born of a mother, guided by my grandmother, who were the only ones of the family to survive the Holocaust. They were truly displaced persons, not refugees: they were not fleeing for a principle that threatened their lives in their country; they had no country or place to go, no verifiable identity. They, like many DPs, were given new papers: birth certificates, religious identities, names, papers for a tight-fisted, antisemitic president, who thought they were Nazi spies and refused to let them in. Think of the SS St. Louis in 1933, forbidden to land in the United States for fear of the evils these thousand Jews threatened: they were forced to turn back and return to Europe, where many of those on this "luxury cruise" (which is how it was billed, but the passengers didn't buy it for a minute: they were refugees) ended up in the death camps, the labor camps, dying just like everyone else. Even Anne Frank, put into a camp, was no more heroic than her fellow inmates, screaming, fighting over bread, soup; dying of typhus two weeks before the camp was liberated. Saintly Anne: no less fractured than anybody else, but fractured in circumstances designed specifically to bring such features out in their many ways.

Fractured, I am a man who is a woman who is a man; a woman who is a man who is a woman. LGBTQ! Peaceful, wanting a quiet, loving family life, and the others who persecute them: they are God's abomination.

Fractured, I am well-educated, but for what matters in my life—writing—I am an autodidact; I am wise, I am a drooling idiot. Disciplined, I am loose, narcissistic: I look to the heavens (if there is such a place; it depends upon your beliefs), but my feet are walking to Sheol. Or is there, in fact, no afterlife, no paradise, purgatory or hell. I'm taking my chances, I know, risking the evil eye, and by the time I know, it'll be too late: I'll either be awash in endless liquid fire, or I'll disappear, soulless: a bit of space dirt.

I am fractured, fractured. I am the hunter and the prey. I am honest and a cheat. And so, in the twilight, in the evening, at the time of night and darkness, I lie alone, or with a companion whom I may or may not know, and come face to face with myself, in a shattered glass.

FREEDOM SONG

In this land, the north wind
brings rain. I look out the
window and see, not barbed
wire, but unmoved rock,
the shadow

of ravens
winging above the trees
dripping as this November day
leads to darkness,
the tumult of the sea

returning,
then silence as the long
night ends and dawn,
within minutes, bursts
into fresh light,

singing, singing.
And I hum along, free
of the remorseless, blaring lights
of the extermination camps:

Free at last, free at last,
Thank God Almighty,
I'm free at last!

Rejoice

Live life live.
Do not hold back.

Sing the song of bliss
As only a mortal can.

Baptize yourself with
Hands full of dirt and ash:

Joy will come again even in loss,
And shovels full of ancient earth

Will tuck us into our narrow house.

Live life live,
And sing with your

Orphic voice the song
Of love the seasons taught.

I will sing and weep;
Weep and sing

Grief in joy, joy
In grief: I live.

I live. Alive. Rejoicing.

Mazel tov mazel tov mazel tov;
Shalom. Shalom. Shalom.

Baruch atah Adonai.

CREDITS

The following pieces have been published in the following journals during the writing of this book in 2018:

Agon, *Mississippi Literary Review*

Wind, Ashes; Evolution; The Bottom of Midnight, *Ink Pantry*

Sequence, *FRIGG Magazine*

Fractures, *Guest Blog in Superstition Review*

Sirje Sets the Town on Fire, *Door is a Jar Review*

Vow; Toivo's Ring; Somewhere By the Sea, *Carbon Culture Review*

Everyday I will Remember
By Christopher Kuhl

No single book or group of books will teach you about the Holocaust, what happened when the Germans decided to cleanse the earth of Jews and Gypsies and Poles and Gays and the people the Germans considered mules or subhumans or devils.

My mother spent 3 years in the concentration camps in Germany. When I would ask her what it was like, she would just say, "If they give you bread, eat it. If they beat you, run away." Unsatisfied, I would press her for more, and when she would finally give in and speak, all she would say was, "You weren't there. You will never understand."

So where does that leave you and me, who weren't in the camps, who will never know what it was like?

It leaves us wondering and asking questions and looking for the answers wherever we can find them. It leaves us reading books by those who survived, great writers like Primo Levi and Elie Wiesel and Viktor Frankel and Wladyslaw Szpilman and Olga Lengyel. And it leaves us reading books by writers who have somehow listened to the voices of those who survived and in those voices heard something that allows them to continue the legacy of those who survived and wrote about it.

Christopher Kuhl is such a writer.

Like the best of them – contemporary poets like Charles Fishman, William Heyen, and Cyrus Cassells – Christopher Kuhl blends stark moments of misery and death with a poetic vision that gives those moments an intensity that we will never forget.

We see this throughout his book **Everyday I Will Remember**. He tells us about those who survived the camps and those who didn't and what they saw and heard: the selections, the ovens, the bayonets in the ribs, the screaming, the diseases, the voices of the German soldiers, the dead children, the mass graves, the boxcars, the empty villages, the electric fences, the bodies piled so high.

But showing us the Holocaust is not all that Christopher Kuhl does. He helps us remember the Holocaust. He does this through his language, his images, his poet's vision. This is most felt I think in those poems in the second half of the book, the section dealing with the time after the war, after the liberation from the camps. In this section, the survivors and the descendants of survivors are themselves seeking the words that will make some sense of the Holocaust.

We see this, for example, in the poem "A Mother's Prayer to Her Son: Remember Me":

I gather the wind
In the palm

Of my hand:

Son of my womb,
Son of my vows,

You have stirred my
Shadow to life....

Christopher Kuhl also brings to his telling of the story of the Holocaust a poet's gift for asking the ultimate questions the Holocaust forces us to ask.

Why did so many die? What do we owe a God who allowed this to happen? Why do such genocides go on and on? Why did the Germans do such terrible things? Do the dead know why they suffered? What is it like to be dead? How should we remember those who suffered?

And why should we remember them?

In an era where people are forgetting the Holocaust and questioning even whether it ever actually occurred, Christopher Kuhl reminds us as only a great poet can why we should never forget.

■ Review by John Guzlowski, author of *Echoes of Tattered Tongues: Memory Unfolded*

About the Reviewer

John Guzlowski's writing appears on Garrison Keillor's *Writers Almanac* and in *Rattle, Ontario Review, North American Review,* and many other journals here and abroad. His poems and personal essays about his Polish parents' experiences as slave laborers in Nazi Germany and refugees after the war appear in his memoir *Echoes of Tattered Tongues* (Aquila Polonica Press). It received the 2017 Benjamin Franklin Poetry Award and the Eric Hoffer Foundation›s Montaigne Award. He is also the author of the Hank and Marvin mystery novels.

Review of Everyday I will Remember
By Lynne Handy

Christopher Kuhl writes "…the act of writing a poem requires the greatest of care, whether dark or sunny, because of its power" on his January 19, 2019 blog. In *Every Day I Will Remember,* he captures stories and images of the Holocaust and after from his scrapbook of memories, shaping them into powerful poems that cannot help but edify and move the reader. Kuhl offers a biographical poem, "Fractures," toward the end of the book, but before we get to page 95, we know the poet and his family well, for we have traveled with them from the Baltic Sea where his grandmother, then young, wears a swim suit, high heels, and holds a frog-shaped float, through the Nazi death camps, and finally to America where his mother, Sirje, a teenager, tantalizes small town boys with her sexy foreignness.

Through his mother's blood, Kuhl is a Jew. Except for his mother and grandmother, his matrilineal side perished in the Holocaust and in Stalinist purges, but he doesn't let his people die. Nor does he let the six million Jews also murdered by the Nazi regime die. He resurrects them, each and every one. In a vision, the prophet Ezekiel beholds a field of human bones. God breathes life into them and as a people, they rise again. Images of bones, symbol of death and resurrection, seed this collection of poems. I feel the poet's anguish in his work, and am grateful he uses *bones* in so many lines, for though they lie in mass graves, as in "Brambly Questions," or are reduced to muddy slurry, as in "The Mud and Bone Garden," they are also a symbol of indestructible life. From "A Blessing":

Bones scattered where once
There was life. And so it goes.

O, threshed and winnowed ones,
Rise up from the earth and know
That you are worth more to Me

Than a thousand sparrows.

Most of the poems are composed in free verse, taking shape when the poet writes the first line. *Fractures* is a prose poem. "Monochrome" is slender; inexorable with its repetition of the word, *gray*. Gray soup, gray potatoes, gray lice, gray bodies. Kuhl's lyrical style links him to his faith: he is the psalmist presiding over dark pastures.

Every Day I Will Remember lives up to its titular promise. Kuhl begins with "Photograph: Baltic Sea (Between the Wars)," a paean to lost family members sunning at the family dacha on the Baltic Sea. The poem ends with the death dates (1939-1945) of five of the people pictured. The final poem in the first section is the tiny, unobtrusive "Epitaph."

dead
I become only
the space
i've left behind

a door ajar
as night crawls
creeps

in

In Part 2: After the War, Kuhl deals with immigration, displacement, and old memories. "Wind, Ashes" tells of the dead who are tied to the motherland and the children born in the new country. "Toivo's Ring" introduces us to Toivo, who gave his wedding ring to his wife when Bolsheviks broke into his house, and abducted and murdered him. The ring was passed on to Kuhl, the last of his line.

One gets the feeling that the poet is sometimes poised between death as a final destination and promises of a heavenly reward. In "The Coming," Jesus will come to the dead who are waiting for him, the tops of their heads facing west. The final poem, "Rejoice," is celebratory: one's time on earth is worth living.

Kuhl doesn't trust the future. The second part begins with an approaching storm, static on the radio, and no one speaking. ("The Gathering Storms.") This reviewer's morning newspaper featured a photo of an Indiana soccer team giving the Nazi salute. In his introduction, Kuhl mentions being heckled by young people as he reads a Holocaust poem at a poetry reading. Most millennials have not heard of the Holocaust. Half the states address genocide education either in grades K-12, or 7 or 8 through 12.

Then there is the remaining half.

The next to the last poem is "Freedom Song." Kuhl ends with the words to an African-American spiritual:

Free at last, free at last,
Thank God Almighty,
I'm free at last.

He can no longer see the *remorseless, blaring lights of the extermination camps.*

Kuhl's poems give illumination to a dark time in mankind's history. *Every Day I Will Remember* should be required reading in every high school genocide class.

CPSIA information can be obtained
at www.ICGtesting.com
Printed in the USA
LVHW010842110319
610189LV00001B/158